A **TRUE** BOOK™

Animals Helping to Detect Diseases

D0846668

SUSAN H. GRAY

Children's Press®
An Imprint of Scholastic Inc.
New York Toronto London Auckland Sydney
Mexico City New Delhi Hong Kong
Danbury, Connecticut

Content Consultant
Dr. Stephen S. Ditchkoff
Professor of Wildlife Sciences
Auburn University
Auburn, Alabama

Library of Congress Cataloging-in-Publication Data
Gray, Susan Heinrichs, author.
 Animals helping to detect diseases / Author, Susan H. Gray.
    pages cm. — (A true book)
 Summary: "Learn how animals can be trained to detect diseases in humans."— Provided by
publisher.
 Audience: Ages 9–12.
 Audience: Grades 4 to 6.
 Includes bibliographical references and index.
 ISBN 978-0-531-21214-1 (library binding : alk. paper) — ISBN 978-0-531-21288-2 (pbk. : alk. paper)
1. Detector dogs—Juvenile literature. 2. Medicine, Preventive—Juvenile literature. 3. Animal train-
ing—Juvenile literature. 4. Working dogs—Juvenile literature. I. Title. II. Series: True book.
 RA436.G73 2015
 636.088'6—dc23   2014030586

© 2015 Scholastic Inc.
All rights reserved. Published in 2015 by Children's Press, an imprint of Scholastic Inc. Published
simultaneously in Canada. Printed in China 62
SCHOLASTIC, CHILDREN'S PRESS, A TRUE BOOK™, and associated logos are trademarks and/or
registered trademarks of Scholastic Inc.
1 2 3 4 5 6 7 8 9 10 R 24 23 22 21 20 19 18 17 16 15

**Front cover: A medical detection dog
checking samples for cancer**

**Back cover: An African giant pouched
rat sniffing samples for tuberculosis**

Find the Truth!

Everything you are about to read is true *except* for one of the sentences on this page.

Which one is **TRUE**?

T or F Rats, mice, and fruit flies are being used to detect diseases.

T or F A dog's nose is about as sensitive to odors as a human's nose.

Find the answers in this book.

3

Contents

THE BIG TRUTH!

Inside a Dog's Nose

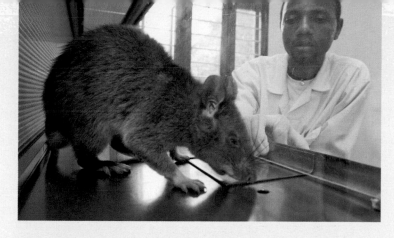

An African giant pouched rat sniffs for disease.

Fruit flies have been used to study diseases in space.

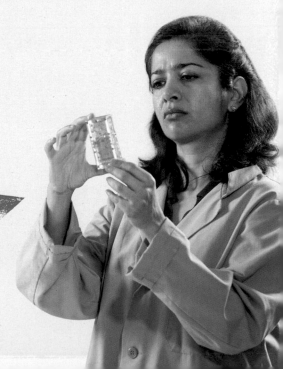

A dog sniffs at a suspicious sample while learning to detect cancer.

CHAPTER 1

Disease Detectives

In Mexico, a doctor is figuring out why a child is dizzy. In India, a lab worker peers at a **vial** of blood. In Florida, a golden retriever sniffs at a jar with fluid in it. In Africa, a rat inhales from a container of air. What is happening in each of these situations? A medical worker is identifying a disease.

In the United States, there are about five doctors for every 2,000 people.

Not Without Problems

To **diagnose** a patient, doctors might order x-rays or blood tests. Sometimes, it takes days to get the results. Often, the tests are very expensive. Therefore, scientists are looking for better ways to make diagnoses.

In some countries, this is especially important. Hospitals are rare. Patients are very unwell by the time they arrive. They need quick diagnoses.

A doctor can learn a lot about a patient's health from a sample of the patient's blood.

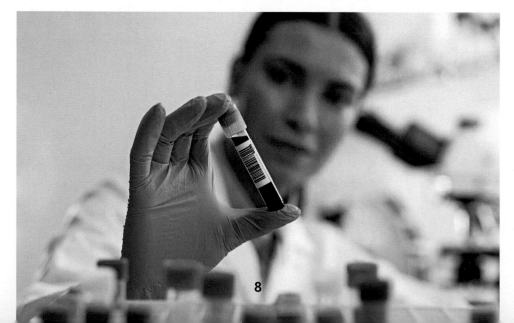

A medic works with a newborn baby in a displaced community in Southeast Asia.

In some countries, five doctors are serving more than 100,000 people.

Often, hospitals in these areas have little money. The newest equipment may not be available. The hospital could be low on testing supplies. There may not be a laboratory nearby. It could take a long time to get test results back. Experts have tried for years to solve these problems. It turns out that some answers were right under their noses.

Hippocrates is often called the father of medicine.

CHAPTER 2

Things Come Together

The science of diagnosis goes back many centuries. Egyptian physician Imhotep diagnosed and treated patients more than 4,600 years ago. Hippocrates, another famous physician, did the same in Greece about 2,400 years ago.

In the 1800s, William Farr of Great Britain became interested in identifying diseases. At the time, doctors did not know exactly why their patients died. Diseases went by many different names and nicknames. This was very confusing.

William Farr's work still impacts medicine today.

Documenting Diseases

Farr wanted medicine to be better organized. He wanted diagnoses to be more orderly. With this in mind, he gathered information from other doctors. Then he made a list of diseases. The list included a description of each illness and the **symptoms** that patients had. Doctors originally used this to identify a person's cause of death. However, this could also be used to diagnose living people.

This idea caught on. Over time, many people added to the knowledge of illnesses. Today, we know about thousands of diseases. We now have specific, standard names for them. For many diseases, we know the causes. Doctors are much better at identifying diseases. Nurses know how they affect patients. Disease detection is not perfect, but it is much more organized.

Diseases used to have names like quinsy and jail fever.

Two medics check on a sick patient.

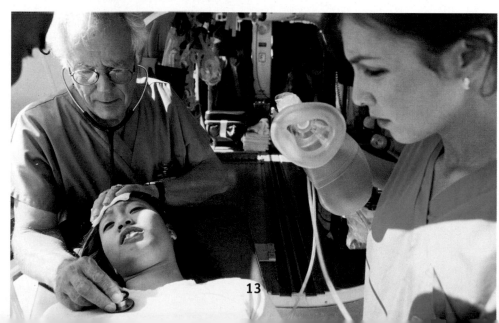

Meanwhile . . .

As medicine was advancing, other fields were, too. People were learning more about animals. They discovered that certain animals had amazing talents. They began putting those talented animals to work.

In England, the police worked with dogs. They saw how dogs could follow scents, so they began using bloodhounds to track down thieves. These dogs helped solve crimes.

Bloodhounds were used in the historic search for Jack the Ripper in London, England, in the late 19th century.

Hunters used bloodhounds more than 800 years ago.

The Saint Bernard gets its name from the mountain pass between Italy and Switzerland where it became famous for rescuing lost travelers.

In Switzerland, **monks** were putting Saint Bernard dogs to work. At first, these large dogs pulled carts. Some also guarded property. But then the monks noticed something. The dogs were not just strong. They also had a great sense of smell. They could find their way home in the snow and could locate travelers who were lost in the mountains. The monks began using Saint Bernards as rescue dogs.

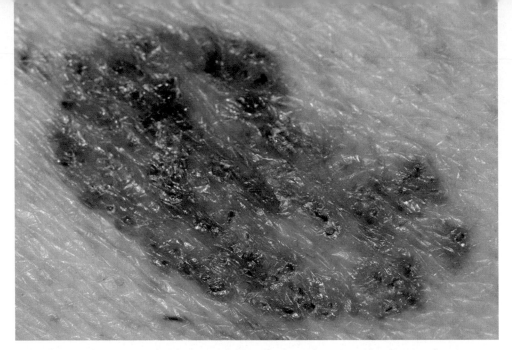

Skin cancer is the most common form of cancer in the United States.

Discovering Other Talents

In the 20th century, Hywel Williams was treating patients in England. He was especially interested in skin diseases. One day, he had a patient with a spot of skin cancer. The patient told Williams an interesting story. Her dog was constantly sniffing the spot. This made her decide to come in for a checkup. The story got Williams thinking. Could dogs detect skin cancer?

Super Smellers

Belgian Bart Weetjens had always liked rats. He knew they were smart and could be trained. He also knew they had an acute sense of smell. At first, he wanted to teach rats to find explosives in old battlefields. Weetjens began his work in 1997. In time, his rats were doing a great job. Then he had another idea. Perhaps rats could detect diseases such as **tuberculosis** (TB), a dangerous lung disease. Again, he was correct! Now, his TB-detecting rats are at work in Africa.

A dog might be trained to lie down or sit down when it smells cancer cells.

CHAPTER 3

Doctor Dogs

Hywel Williams thought a lot about his patient's dog. He knew that dogs have a good sense of smell. Perhaps any dog could sniff out skin cancer.

In time, more doctors became interested in this idea. They began testing dogs. They wanted to see if dogs could find other types of cancer, too. With every new test, the dogs proved they could. They sniffed out lung, skin, bladder, and other cancers.

The moisture on a dog's nose helps capture odors in the air.

What's Going On?

What exactly do the dogs smell? They probably smell **volatile organic compounds**, known as VOCs. Volatile materials evaporate quickly. Organic compounds contain carbon and other atoms.

When VOCs evaporate, their molecules disperse into the air. People cannot smell very small amounts of VOCs, but dogs can. Williams's patient with skin cancer was very lucky. Her dog smelled VOCs on her skin and would not leave her alone.

A dog's sensitive nose can pick up scents a human never notices.

A lot of the VOCs in the air come from plants.

Many VOCs have a strong smell. Gasoline, for example, is a VOC. Fingernail polish remover is also one. The smells of a new car are probably from VOCs.

Those are man-made compounds. But VOCs also exist in nature. Plants give off plenty of them, but most people do not notice. Animals give them off, too. Diseased tissues also release VOCs. These natural VOCs are the ones that dogs detect so well.

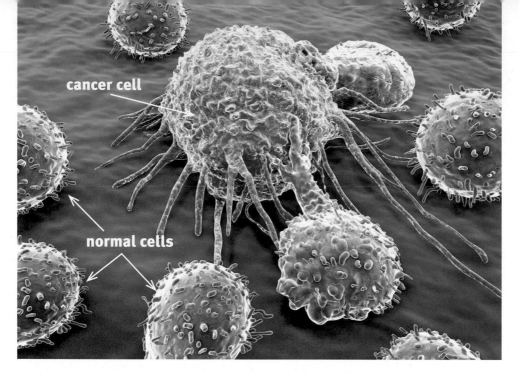

cancer cell

normal cells

Because cancer cells are so different from normal cells, they have a different smell.

Cancer cells act differently than normal cells. Cancer cells multiply rapidly and **emit** particular VOCs. The VOCs might show up in a patient's breath. They might be present around a spot on the skin. They might even appear in a patient's urine. Perhaps they are in sweat, earwax, and tears. There are all sorts of places where VOCs might show up.

Dogs on Duty

Today, dogs are used to detect lung and breast cancer. They do this simply by smelling a patient's breath. They are trained to sit or lie down when they sense cancer VOCs. Dogs can also detect bladder cancer. To do this, they sniff just a tiny bit of a patient's urine.

Dogs are amazingly good at this. They are very accurate and quite fast. They also work cheaply!

Dogs that detect diseases are called medical detection dogs.

The dog will sit by the sample that she detects has cancer.

Other Illnesses

Dogs can do more than detect cancer. They can tell when a patient is low on sugar. They also know when someone is about to have a **seizure**. In these cases, they might smell VOCs, but they also might notice other things. Perhaps they see that someone is getting shaky. Maybe they hear changes in a person's voice. They alert people by nudging them or by barking.

Service dogs such as seizure alert dogs form close relationships with their humans.

24

Medical detection dogs start their training at only 8 weeks old.

Dogs in England are being trained to find bedbugs.

Dogs have yet another talent. They can smell germs. Hospitals always try to keep germs under control, but some germs are very tough to get rid of.

Dogs can smell germs in the air and can tell which patients are carrying them. These dogs are very helpful. They show nurses which patients need more care. They can also show which rooms need a good cleaning.

Inside a Dog's Nose

What makes dog noses so special? Why can dogs smell things that people cannot? One reason is that dogs have more cells that detect scents. Humans have only 5 million or 6 million of these cells. Dogs have between 200 million and 300 million! Also, our brains are different. Everyone has a brain area that analyzes smells. However, in dogs, this section makes up a larger portion of the brain than it does in humans.

Dog and human nostrils are different, too. We cannot wiggle our nostrils the way dogs wiggle theirs. Dogs can turn their nostrils sideways one at a time. In doing this, the nose picks up smells from two different directions. That helps the dog know where odors are coming from.

Scientists are trying to learn more about dog noses. They hope to understand how a dog's nose can detect disease.

CHAPTER 4

Other Animals Get Involved

Dogs are not the only animals with medical jobs. Rats, mice, and flies are hard at work, too. Rats can sniff out the germ that causes tuberculosis, or TB. TB is very common in some African countries. The rats being used to detect it are also very common in Africa. But these are no ordinary rats. They are African giant pouched rats.

It takes between 6 to 12 months of training for the African giant pouched rats to learn how to detect TB.

A rat walks along a line of samples, sniffing for evidence of TB.

The rats' reward usually contains mashed bananas.

What the Rats Do

This is how rats do their work. First, they must be trained. In training, rats smell two different kinds of samples: fluids with the TB germs, and fluids without. The rats scratch around a sample each time they smell the germ. When they are correct, they get a reward. Only the best rats go on to work in hospitals as disease detectors.

At the hospital, they work in a lab. Doctors collect fluid from their patients' lungs. The fluid goes into little containers. Next, a trained rat is brought in. The rat sniffs the containers. After sniffing each container, the rat either scratches or moves on. Lab workers note which containers made the rats scratch. This way, doctors know which patients have TB.

An African giant pouched rat gets its name from the pouches in its cheeks.

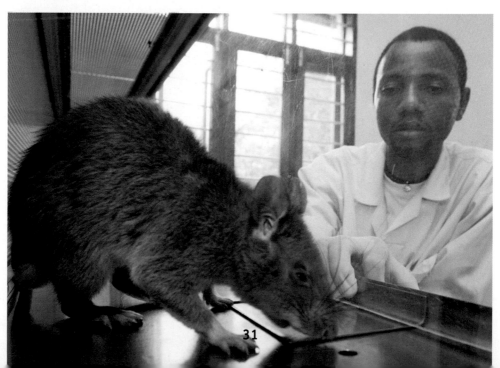

Without rats, lab workers find TB by dyeing fluid samples and looking at them under a microscope. This process is slow and not very accurate. There must be many TB germs present or lab workers will miss them. In addition, areas of Africa have few hospitals. They may be short on lab workers or equipment. African giant rats take only a few seconds to find TB germs without dye or microscopes.

Heating a glass slide containing a fluid sample helps highlight any evidence of TB.

Rats in Action

African pouched rats have found quite a bit of success in Africa. Since 2008, the rats have screened more than 200,000 samples in Dar es Salaam, Tanzania. They found about 5,000 TB cases that human screeners missed. In Maputo, Mozambique, the rats have been in use since 2013. In their first year, they found an extra 556 TB cases in the nearly 20,000 samples they screened.

Avian flu could potentially destroy a chicken farm.

The first known case of a person getting avian flu was in 1997.

Sniffing Out Avian Flu

Mice are catching up with dogs and rats. Mice can identify birds with **avian** flu. This is a disease that spreads from bird to bird. The flu can kill chickens, turkeys, and pet birds. It can spread through chicken farms, destroying their chicken populations. It can also infect people, making them sick.

Mice can identify infected birds by their droppings. No one knows exactly what the mice smell. It is probably VOCs. But trained mice can become quite good at this.

Mice could someday be on the front lines against this disease. They might be able to sniff out the first sick duck in a city park. They might find the one infected bird at the zoo. This could keep the disease from spreading.

Mice, like many animals, have a very good sense of smell.

The Smallest Workers

Fruit flies are tiny—not much bigger than pinheads. However, they detect diseases just like dogs and rats do. Like these other animals, fruit flies detect VOCs.

Fruit flies do not have noses, but they can still smell things. They use their **antennae**. These organs pick up odors in the air. This helps the fly find fruit. And that's not all. Different odors cause the antennae to change colors.

A microscope is needed for a good look at a fruit fly and its antennae.

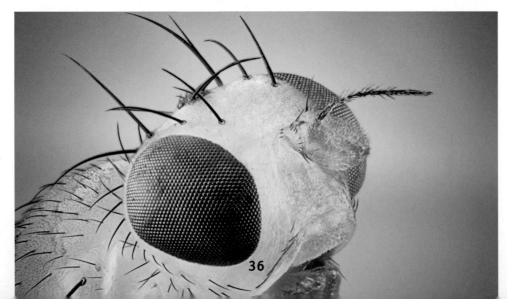

Ripe fruits emit VOCs.

A group of scientists wanted to study these flies. They wondered about the flies' sense of smell. Could the flies smell VOCs in cancer cells? If so, would their antennae change color? How could someone see those colors? After all, it is hard to see anything on these tiny flies. The scientists thought a long time. How could they answer these questions?

The scientists decided to use a microscope with a special light on it. They put the fruit flies under the microscope. The light made their antennae colors show up really well.

Next, the scientists blew air over the flies. Some was air that had been around cancer cells. Some was air that had been around normal cells.

Timeline of Medical Diagnosis

About 430 B.C.E.
Hippocrates works as a doctor in Greece.

About 1670 C.E.
Saint Bernards begin to be used in rescue work in the Alps.

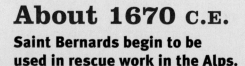

The scientists watched closely. They saw the antennae change colors. Antennae had one color pattern in the normal air. They had another pattern in the air exposed to cancer.

The flies could show the difference! They did not have to be trained. No one had to give them rewards. Their antennae colors changed automatically. The scientists were excited. Flies had detected VOCs from cancer cells.

1830s to 1870s
William Farr improves descriptions of diseases.

2008
Bart Weetjens begins using rats to detect tuberculosis.

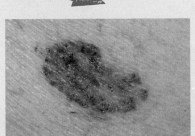

1989
Hywel Williams publishes an article about a cancer patient's dog.

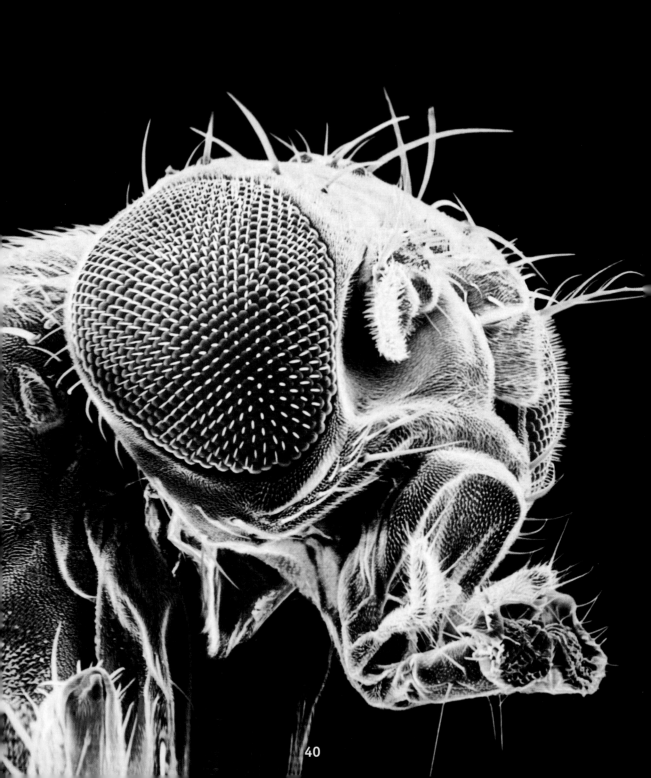

CHAPTER 5

Coming Soon

Scientists are looking at more ways to use dogs, rats, and mice. One day, these animals might be used to detect many types of cancer. Maybe they will be finding other diseases.

Fruit flies are also getting more attention. Some experts think they can grow "smarter" flies. Maybe these flies will even glow when they come near cancer cells.

Fruit flies are cheap and easy to keep in a lab.

An e-nose was sent into space on the International Space Station for several months to study the spacecraft's air supply.

New Detectors

Scientists are also testing bees. These insects learn quickly. They can learn to respond to certain smells. Perhaps they can be put to use detecting VOCs.

Some experts are creating "electronic noses." These machines are able to sense tiny amounts of VOCs. Some e-noses have already been built. They analyze the gases in a patient's breath and can detect lung cancer.

It is possible that many labs will use e-noses someday. However, e-noses might be too expensive for some hospitals. There may also be problems shipping them to some countries.

On the other hand, rats, mice, and dogs are everywhere. They are very accurate in their medical work. They work for small rewards. Because of this, animals will continue to be used to detect diseases for years to come. ★

Some scientists say that dogs are still more accurate than current e-noses.

Number of deadly diseases on William Farr's list: 27

Number of lives saved by Saint Bernard dogs in the Alps: About 2,000

Number of new cases of TB in the world in 2012: 8.6 million

Biggest producers of VOCs: Plants

Biggest source of man-made VOCs: The transportation industry

Time it takes a dog to sniff out germs in a hospital ward: About 10 minutes

African countries using rats to find TB: Tanzania and Mozambique

Did you find the truth?

Rats, mice, and fruit flies are being used to detect diseases.

A dog's nose is about as sensitive to odors as a human's nose.

Resources

Books

Goldish, Meish. *Dogs*. New York: Bearport Publishing, 2007.

Ruffin, Frances. *Medical Detective Dogs*. New York: Bearport Publishing, 2006.

Visit this Scholastic Web site for more information on animals helping to detect diseases:

★ www.factsfornow.scholastic.com
Enter the keywords **Animals Helping to Detect Diseases**

Important Words

antennae (an-TEN-ee) — feelers on the head of an insect

avian (AY-vee-uhn) — relating to birds

diagnose (dye-uhg-NOHS) — to determine what disease a patient has or what the cause of a problem is

emit (i-MIT) — to produce or send out something such as heat, light, signals, or sound

monks (MUHNGKS) — men who live apart from society in a religious community according to strict rules

seizure (SEE-zhur) — a sudden attack or spasm

symptoms (SIMP-tuhmz) — signs of an illness

tuberculosis (too-bur-kyuh-LOH-sis) — a highly contagious disease caused by bacteria that usually affects the lungs

vial (VYE-uhl) — a very small glass or plastic container

volatile organic compounds (VAH-luh-tile or-GAN-ik KAHM-powndz) — chemicals that evaporate quickly into the air

Index

Page numbers in **bold** indicate illustrations.

About the Author

Susan H. Gray has a master's degree in zoology and has written more than 140 reference books for children. She especially likes to write about animals and on topics that engage children in science. She and her husband, Michael, live in Cabot, Arkansas.